Days of the Exodusters

by Corrine Wenthworth • illustrated by E. Wolf

Harcourt

Orlando   Boston   Dallas   Chicago   San Diego

Visit *The Learning Site!*

www.harcourtschool.com

In the year of eighteen seventy-nine,
A fever spread throughout the land.
Not a fever that makes the head hot
And the body ache. This fever was a dream
That spread through a people.
This fever was caught by many
Who longed for a life of freedom
And an opportunity to own and farm the land.

African Americans were on the move—
They gathered together, families and friends.
Through their talk, the fever spread
And the journey was no longer a dream.
Together they began the long march west,
To answer the call of the open land.
A place called Kansas beckoned them,
Thousands and many thousands more.

In the Exodus in days of old,
So it is that the story goes,
A man named Moses led his folk
To the fertile land, a better life.
So, too, did African Americans march,
As Exodusters they were known.
To the promised land of Kansas they went,
To a fertile land, this was their dream.

The Civil War had brought freedom at last.
After years of shackles and service,
These men and women deserved a new start.
So the U.S. government offered the chance
To settle some land on the wide open plains.
For African Americans, this was an opportunity
To leave the shadow of someone else's fields,
An opportunity to enjoy their own harvest.

America was proud to offer this gift
To men and women new to freedom.
The land was promised to any and all
Who agreed to homestead at least five years.
All that it cost was a five-dollar fee
And five long years of backbreaking toil.
For African Americans, toil was not new,
But to own land was a dream come true.

Some came by wagon, some came on foot,
Some came by steamboat, some by rail.
The Exodusters left the South behind,
And to Kansas they came any way they could.
In their minds an image was taking shape—
The image of the black pioneer.
Yes, the African American pioneer
Was about to tame the wild frontier.

The "Kansas Fever Exodus" it was called,
As Exodusters flocked to the promised land.
The time was at hand to begin again,
And many came, and many stayed.
What possibilities did this Kansas extend
For building a life in a western state?
The possibilities were to work in the towns
Or homestead out on the open plains.

Some Exodusters were city folk—
Homesteading, they said, was not for them.
In eastern Kansas, to the towns they came
To find the jobs that fit their skills.
Those who planned to work and till the land
Headed for the western Kansas plains.
There to fulfill their dreams, they said,
By homesteading in that promised land.

In western Kansas, the Exodusters found
Parcels of land for placing their claims.
They had come so far and survived it all.
Now new struggles were about to begin.
As all pioneers, they were soon to learn
The hardship of building life on the plains.
But they learned to live in harmony
And made this place into their home.

Shelter was the first task at hand,
Yet wood for building was very scarce.
So Exodusters used what they could find
And built their homes with bricks of sod.
The topmost layer of prairie soil
Was made of tangled roots of grass.
Sod, matted and tough, they cut into slabs,
Forming bricks with which to build new homes.

Try to imagine what life was like
For the Exodusters on the plains.
"Soddies" they named their homes.
Sod covered the land they used to farm.
Iron plows broke on the sod-covered ground,
So tough on a plow, only steel did the job.
Backbreaking work done by one and all.
Only the strong could survive such a life.

Some days on the plains were really fine,
When all of life was in harmony.
When grass smelled sweet, and air was soft,
And the plains rolled away to meet the sky.
But then came the times of drought, of flood,
Of blizzards, and sweeping prairie fires.
And worst of all, perhaps, were the plagues
Of grasshoppers eating up the plains.

Here and there across the Kansas plains,
Towns sprang up, like flowers in spring.
In the towns were general stores and such,
Where pioneers could stock up on supplies.
Some Exodusters chose to move on.
Some even returned to the South they knew.
Of all the towns these pioneers built,
Only Nicodemus remains today.

Those who settled Nicodemus
Stayed, worked hard, and prospered at times.
Sod home gave way to limestone house,
Then wooden house, with porch and arbor.
Father returns from work, and children
Return from school as Mother prepares
A meal made from the fruits of their harvest.
The taste of freedom is ever so sweet.

This fever that had brought them west
Was a fever that healed a broken people.
Success was theirs at last, and the fever
Of a dream had led the way to a new life.
A pioneer would have smiled at the sight
Of the free smile of a man who owns land.
A pioneer would have smiled at the sight,
Back in the days of the Exodusters.